EXPRESSIONS OF A SINGLE WOMAN

Dating without Discrimination

BY NICHELLE A. HODGE

ISBN-13: 978-1-970079-51-7

Published and edited by:
Opportune Independent Publishing Co.
113 N. Live Oak Street
Houston, TX 77003
(832) 263-1700
www.opportunepublishing.com

Ladies in waiting, you may or may not be able to relate to the characters in this book. However, you may find humor and or even agree as to why it's sometimes best to date yourself for a season or few…

Not all of the relationships have the same results. We all have things we're willing to sacrifice, while there are other areas of compromise. Yet, I refuse to give up on my desire to have a successful and meaningful relationship, that lasts a lifetime with my future husband, and I hope that you won't either.

Acknowledgements

I acknowledge my Lord and Savior, Jesus Christ. It is because of my acceptance of, belief in, and acting upon the Word of God, that I am an Overcomer. All that I've had to endure has been for a purpose. Through the pain, I was made whole. Every tear that I've shed has not gone without notice.

One of my all-time favorite promises is found in ***Psalm 27:10***, and I remind God of it often. This promise has been fulfilled many times over, and for that, I am eternally grateful.

I would also like to acknowledge my son, Jeremiah Hodge, who endured the growing pains of his mom. He is truly a God send. His temperament balances me much.

To my sisters who've lived through some of the struggles too. Thank God that we don't look like what we've been through! To my friends who've provided wise counsel, been a listening ear, a shoulder to cry on, and even pieces of iron who help keep me accountable and sharp to continue on this journey. Many blessings for your faithfulness.

To all who have provided a covering spiritually along the way, please know that I believe in putting the Word to work. It's more than believing and shouting Amen. "How will I apply what you've said to my life?" "Am I growing in my walk with Christ?" "Is there fruit in my life because of the seeds you planted?" I have purposely set out to be better than who I was. Each day I get to keep working toward greatness. Even though I've stumbled along the way, I've gotten back up, and now with steady steps, I walk by faith. There is fruit in abundance. By your example, I can continue to sow seeds for Kingdom causes. Hallelujah! AMEN

Table of Contents

What Are You Really Looking For?

You say you want a good woman...

Yet I'm sure you've walked by many.

She may not be all that you're looking for, but do you

expect her to meet your every need!?!

It's impossible!

Let God be the sole provider...

When you see her, be willing to accept all that she is,

and choose to love her intentionally, unconditionally,

and unapologetically.

Say what you mean and prove what you say...

She'll respect you for it and treat you like the king she

knows you are!

Introduction

The ‘What Are You Really Looking For?’ was included under my “In A Nutshell” bio on a dating website that I rejoined to help meet a comparable and compatible man. Less than a thirty day trial period, I deleted my profile. I won’t discourage you and say that this way of meeting individuals was unsuccessful. I’ve had the opportunity of meeting some interesting people. After spending some time, I learned that what is valuable and important to me at this stage in my life was not so much to those I had come across.

I've tried dating in different season of my life. The results have been successful failures. The process of learning about another human being can be emotional, timely, and even costly. I'm going to share with you what I've encounter on this road to companionship.

It took courage, but I wanted to be transparent and share some of my truth with you as it relates to dating. Remember to set boundaries, be open and honest about your needs and expectations, never forget to keep all lines of communication open, and most of all have fun.

BE-YOU-To the-FULLest! Believe that you are enough!

First Love, or So I Thought

Can you really be in love at fourteen? Here I was, free from the rules and restrictions of my mother's home, dating…

I remember writing a note to a popular boy in middle school and instead of giving the letter to him, I ripped it into pieces and threw it in the trash. My mom found it and she gave me a talking to. "I send you to school to learn, not to chase after no pissy-tail boy!" I knew she was only trying to save me from a heartache that I was not prepared for. Well, I wanted to learn alright, and I didn't think the school could teach me what I was trying to find out.

My first love interest was sixteen, just two years older than me. He was tall, had a bright smile, and made me laugh. He was also Puerto Rican, who moved from Brooklyn, NY. I loved to hear his accent! How he carried himself was what attracted me to him. He was my *novio* and I was his *linda novia*.

We didn't get to see much of each other during the week due to the fact that we lived in different parts of the city. On the weekend we'd meet up at a mutual friend's house or at the park. We'd talk and laugh for hours. I looked forward to spending time with him. He knew how to make me feel special.

When you're young and dumb, that combination can be a disaster. Pride and selfishness can destroy you too.

The more time I spent with my '*Papi*', the more confident I'd become. We could be silly together and it didn't matter, as long as we were in each other's company. Then…

Those sweet nothings he'd whisper to me, became just that. I'd see him less and less. I was concerned enough to ask our friends what was up, but no one knew, since they were involved in their own love triangles. Anyway, I hoped for the best.

We didn't have cell phones back then to call or send a quick text. We had pagers and pay phones, and without access to any, time would reveal why his presence grew scarce.

One night we decided to go to a house party that was close to our normal hangout spot. My home girl was trying her best to get my attention. After murmuring a few words in my ear, she pointed me in the direction that I needed to look… I couldn't believe my eyes! Instantly my tears fell, not of pain, but of burning anger. Here goes my *Papi* booed up with some other chic. I was livid and I wanted him to know what was on my mind. I marched over to him and put some space between the two lovebirds. After giving him a piece of my mind, I stormed out of the party, headed home, with my heart ice cold.

I was never a girl to take revenge. I believe, to this day, that what goes around, comes around and around.

The pain that I felt at that moment was different to what I was used to. This wasn't the result of any disciplinary action. It was because of rejection. Yea, I was disrespected, but I reacted by telling him that what he did to me, to us, was not cool.

The thought of not being wanted, I didn't know how to process that. The anger that I felt would be carried around for years. I'd mask it well, pretending that everything was okay.

I made myself unavailable to my friends, just so I could suffer in silence. I didn't want any pity and I didn't want to chance running into him ever again…

However, a few year later, when I was visiting with a mutual friend, I seen a familiar face in the hall. My heart leaped, but I shrugged it off. It can't be him. He calls my name, I freeze. Turning around, he starts walking toward me. Emotions came rushing to me, so I held my breath since I didn't know how to react. He apologizes for hurting me that night. "I never meant to hurt you!" "I'm sorry! Will you forgive me!?!" Those words melted my heart enough to exhale. I said I forgave you a long time ago. Smiling, I went on my way…

I was free to explore the world of love again. How would it greet me the next time around? Would I recognize it? Would I entertain it? Maybe, maybe not!

Expressions of a Single Woman

Running out on love is when I no longer submit
myself to you, even though I wanted to be yours.
The only one!
Not another option, but a final choice.
Well, it's not just your decision...
My love will not last on a revolving door.
For soon my heart will read "Do Not Disturb!"
or "Under Construction!"
Which will be okay to repair any brokenness
before moving onto the Real Thing.
I believe that there is a man for whom I am just
enough.

The Father Figure

There is nothing like the love of father, or so I've heard. Unfortunately, I never remembered looking at my biological father's face. He left my mother when we were only two years old. Living in Tortola, BVI – it was there we got news that he died just before we turned sixteen. The news was devastating! How could this be a part of God's plan!?! So many questions to ask, but now there would be no answer. Was it that longing in me to be loved by my dad that pushed me into the arms of an older man for comfort, protection, and validation?

When you are searching for something that you can't quite identify, be careful… What finds you may be someone or thing that you aren't ready to deal with.

Returning to the Caribbean after graduating high school was an adjustment. I had the opportunity to be reconciled with my mother. We made peace with one another. I learned to forgive, love, and honor her.

After moving a few places, we began to stabilize. We now lived on Soldiers Hill. I had a decent job not far from town. When I wasn't working, I spent a lot of time walking around the island. One day walking past the track and field grounds across from the police station and primary school, a green jeep begins to slow down. A man rolls down his window, says a few words that make me smile, then he reaches for my face, kissing me on the lips, he drives off. Who, what!?! I was stunned. Also blushing. What kind of man would do something so forward!?!

He was a bold man! Twice my age too. I was nineteen when he began to court me. He was also known to be a ladies man, who eventually ended up with who and what he wanted. Boi'dem island men! He really was a grown man! That's right! I thought I needed one too. He was a boss! Had businesses, money, reputation… He indeed was somebody! He was also caring, thoughtful, and considerate.

In the mornings, he would bring me breakfast at work. In the afternoons, we'd go for drives around the island and stop for frozen virgin daiquiris. When he was off island doing business, he'd return with a gift or two. He made me feel special! Now, it's one thing to make your own money and treat yourself, but when you're man takes time to show his appreciation of and toward you, it makes you feel all warm and tingly.

Our relationship was getting serious. Yet, others who noticed would comment and try to discourage me. I accepted him for who he was and didn't care what people said about him. My mother even disapproved, but it was my lesson to learn.

After work one afternoon, I came home and took a nap. He came looking for me. He blew his horn, but I didn't answer. This was the normal routine if I made it home before we'd go out. He blew the horn again, and after not seeing me, he boldly knocked on my mother's front door asking for me. What!?! Who does that!?! He did that!!! My mother came into the room and woke me up. She told me that some man was looking for me. She knew of him, but like everyone else, she wanted to warn me of him too. I was blinded by love, and again, I didn't want anyone to take that away from me.

I was afraid of what my mom might do, but I rebelled anyway. Before leaving the house, she gave me her final warning. "If you don't leave that man, let him find a place for you to stay!" She meant every word! Then she made a statement that I certainly hadn't thought of. "What if you come home pregnant?!?" I wasn't even thinking about having kids at that moment. I just wanted to get to my man…

So, I left. Running down the stairs, jumping into the waiting jeep. Before pulling off, I looked at this bold man and thought he was crazy. You knocked on my mother's door!?! Don't you know she could've knocked you down!?!

After hanging out with each other for most of the night, he dropped me home. I thought that I was going to shower and go to bed. Wrong! My mother locked me out the house… So I slept on the front porch. When she opened the door in the morning, I told her my decision. Thanks mom, but I'm leaving. There I go trying to be grown. When a young girl thinks she's grown, she can no longer live in her mother's house. Only one Queen for the castle allowed.

I was on a desperate search for this man. I caught a ride to Joe's Hill Road. Once I found him, I shared my plight, and waited. He told him to give me until the end of the day and he'd have me straight. There was no invitation to stay with him at home. He found me a place to live and even made sure to have it furnished. He also agreed to take or the rent and utilities.

Here I am at nineteen, working, and with my own place. I thought I was grown! Acting and being grown is entirely two different things!

My quaint little place was quiet. I had cable, but most days I'd just go home and be by myself. He'd come to check on me during the week. He let himself in since he had a key.

The excitement that I had with first leaving home was gone. Our outings were less and less. I left the safety and comforts of my mother's home to place house, with a grown man. I began to resent him. How could you have me out here by myself in the middle of nowhere?

One day my neighbor reached out to me to let me know that my electricity bill was late. When I questioned him about it, he promised to take care of it. He did... but I started feeling neglected. I humbled myself, calling my mother asking to return home. She shared some words of wisdom, and after forgiving me of my foolish indiscretion, she welcomed me back home.

I arranged a ride to bring my things back to my mother's house up Soldiers Hill. I told this grown man that I was unhappy and didn't want to be in a relationship any longer. He didn't object. Time passed and I knew that it'd be hard to date anyone after him. He was a man of high regard. We were cordial when we'd see each other around the island. I was happy back at home, keeping to myself.

He made it his business to let me know that he still had feelings for me. As did I. I moved home, but he still had a place in my heart. No man had ever taken the time to show me that he cared for me the way that he did. Nor were there any ever supportive of my decisions, no matter how foolish they seemed.

The love affair was back in motion. This time around, we were discreet. We were like two little school age kids playing a game. Only, love is not a game. To abuse and misuse love can be fatal.

The statement that my mother spoke the night before I left home came back to haunt me. We were somewhat safe when we were together. One night of passion changed my whole life. I got pregnant at nineteen!

What had seemed like a beautiful fantasy, quickly turned into a scary nightmare. I shared the news with him and he denied the fact that we were ever together. Again, I was heartbroken. No pain that I've felt up to this point. Yes, I've suffered physically, had scars, but this was my first pregnancy! I've never had a baby before. I wasn't even sure that I was ready to be a mom, let alone be a single parent.

I had morning sickness for a few months before even confirming my pregnancy. I resigned from my job, bought a one way ticket to return to Georgia, USA. Once I got settled in, I wrote my mother a letter to inform her of my current state. As if she didn't know!?! I was surprised that she wrote back. She let me know that when we make decisions, we have to deal with the consequences. She didn't approve of my carelessness, but she didn't love me any less.

When you're in love with a man nearly twice your age, you're not prepared for the type of games they play. Their experiences are no match with the milk on your breath. Since I had to be a single mother, I'd rely on the support around me to help raise our son. Oh how I wish he was a father to my son. That however, was only a dream.

I will always love this man for the gift that was given to me through his loins. Our son is a fine young man that I hope he has a chance to meet before his days are gone.

Expressions of a Single Woman

Respect.

Admiration.

Love for a lifetime was my (wish) intent.

Yet, life teaches you to give it all to the one who shows you their intent is equal to yours.

Fatal Attraction

I can honestly say that throughout my life, I've not been afraid to try many different things, at least one. Even in relationships, I was not close minded about location, race, or socioeconomic status. However, there is a reason to have a good level of fear in your life. In fear of God, we reverence Him. In fear of authority, we obey. In fear of others, we treat them with mutual respect…

The love that I've known thus far has been Hispanic, Italian, West Indian, Northern, Western, Eastern, and Southern. I've dated a younger man, at least by a two to three year difference. Older men, nearly twice my age. Neither stage meant maturity or even a sincere readiness of commitment. I believe that dating is to collect data, a chance to grow as an individual, and to prepare oneself for marriage, a lifetime commitment – should and when an opportunity presents itself.

By now, traveling had become a normal part of my life.

The place: California.

The man: Mysterious.

Being an inquisitive rebel, I was attracted to a man who was enigmatic. There would be something about him that I just had to find out about. Maybe it was altogether his swag. I couldn't quite put my finger on it…

Our meeting was brief, but unforgettable. He was a fair skinned brother with hazel eyes. Maybe it was that feature that mesmerized me. My stay in the West was temporary. Before heading back home, we agreed that we would keep in touch. We made big plans during our long distance calls.

One particular afternoon, I received a very disturbing phone call from a complete stranger about this man. The message was a warning that no good would come of this relationship. Although he sounded sweet and the promises he made were grand, his intentions toward me were anything less than. I've known fear, but this kind was unsettling to the point that I shuddered. There I was, standing still, but a new set of senses on full alert. I didn't ignore the message that was given to me that day, but kept it at the forefront of my mind.

Months after that call, I receive a letter in the mail from this young man's father. He heard about me through his son and wanted me to be aware of how things were going. He apologized for being the bearer of bad news. The authorities found his son's body dead, in a hotel somewhere in Mexico. He didn't provide any other details, but assured me that he thought it was best for me to know.

Only God knows why I received that phone call and the disturbing news that followed shortly after. Seeing that I was hard of hearing, maybe this would cause me to slow down and not be so trusting. Wisdom and discernment is something that I've heard of, but didn't quite understand that I could ask for it, and use it in all of my relationships.

When there would be failure in this area of my life, I'd just refocus on parenting, education, or my career. I'd make excuses to not try again. That would only work for so long.

Expressions of a Single Woman

We've met before...

I'm sure of it!

How can we react to one another the way we do,

in this short period of time?

Well, one thing I am certain of...

This time, I'm not letting you go!

Opportunists

Who wouldn't want to take advantage of an opportunity presented to them? I most certainly would! When it comes to dating, you may not be sure of what you end up with. Giving your all doesn't guarantee that the return on your investment will be favorable.

This topic is three-fold, so please be patient with me as I share briefly about what I've encountered from men who only want to receive, and not give genuinely what they're asking for.

Who remembers Black Planet? This was the beginning of social media, and had a little bit more class than My Space. Create your profile, set your location to meet people of color near you – in hopes to network and/or have lasting, meaningful relationships.

Online anything, means – ***AT YOUR OWN RISK!*** There are success stories of people who've met online, got married, have kids, and are still together, working on that happily ever – sometimes story.

This brother had potential. He was a paralegal at a prestigious law firm in Boston, MA. That was the place of our initial meet once we chatted online. We agreed to go to a First Friday event and make it official. Our first meeting was fun. We danced the night away. Cellphones were in use and we kept in frequent contact. Since he lived in Lynn, MA we had to find a mutual place to hang out. Once we could agree on a place, we'd make our time together worthwhile.

Because of his line of work, our conversations would be stimulating. A man who is articulate, is an attractive man. A man of many words, is also a lying man. A man who lies frequently is a dangerous man. Telling so many stories, he starts to think of them as truth. Shame on a naïve women who believes the words that come out of his mouth.

His story: I'm in a bind and I need some help.

My response: What kind of help do you need?

His story: I need some money to clear up this 'thing'...

RED FLAG

My response: I'll see what I can do...

Now, I've done some foolish things in the name of love. I admit that LOVE HAD NOTHING

TO DO WITH THIS NEXT MOVE… I worked a few things around and wrote him a check to ‘help’ him out. I regretted the decision, but against my better judgement, went through with believing his lies. Do you know what he did with the money? He bought a damn motorcycle! That’s right! STUPID me! We fell out and I wanted to ride full speed over him with that bike. More so, I wanted to kick my dumb self for being not listening to my first mind.

I don’t oppose giving someone financial assistance when they’re in dire need. I do object to giving in to irresponsible, careless, and manipulative adults who play on the weaknesses of others. Was the lesson learned? I guess not! Another financial test would come years later. It is said that if you fail a test, you have to go through it again. The next time around is harder.

This second test caught me off guard. I wasn't interested in dating anyone at this time. I was focusing on crucifying my flesh and growing spiritually. Once saved, always saved. Though a man or woman falls, he or she can rise again. That's what I believed when I got saved as a child, and that's what I still believe!

While attending a leadership conference at church, I see a familiar face. During a session, we kept making eye contact. Throughout the day, we'd end up being in most of the same courses. I could feel the energy when we looked at each other. He'd stare. I'd look. He'd turn away, and vice versa. As we were leaving our last session before lunch, he reached out to me, exchanged a few words, and we met up for lunch. This time, I was ready. I gave him my business card and tried my best to focus on what was being taught for the rest of the day.

The conference had ended and life went on. What seemed like a long time would only be a few days until my phone would ring. I missed the call, but there was no message. I waited to see if he'd call again. An hour later, I try the number back, but there was no answer. I heard his voice and smiled to myself, leaving a message. Not wanting to play phone tag, I turned up the volume so I could hear the ringtone, and kept the phone attached to my hip for the rest of the day. When he finally returned my call, I tried to act as if I wasn't excited to hear from him.

There's excitement in having something or someone new. You go through the moments of communicating for hours, to wanting to spend every available moment together. That's fine when you're in your late teens and early twenties. When you reach your late thirties, you start to make time for what matters most. At least you put in some effort, so much time isn't wasted.

In the process of getting to know this man, he was in a period of transition - physically, relationally, and financially. I should have let it be known that he came with a lot from the beginning and kept moving on my way without getting too involved. A saying I heard rang true in my ears, "who don't hear, does feel!" I wanted to be there for him, as someone whom he could trust.

One evening before going out, we stopped by his mother's place to drop something off. He introduced me to his mom. A mother knows her child. She shared some words that I didn't take the time hear, but in time would recall those words with contempt.

We spent some time together for my birthday and had a nice time. But it cost me. Having been through a period of abuse in my life, when it came to relationships with men, I knew to speak up when I felt uncomfortable. Things were starting to get better for him, but it still cost me. There was some control issues that put me on alert. Questioning the length of my telephone conversations became a bit much. Then it was gripe about who I allowed in my home. Wait a minute now! I'd cook some great meals, make sure to invite you, but you always decline… and now you trying to tell me who can't come by the house that I'm responsible for!?! I have a feeling that this isn't going to end well, but everyone deserves another chance, right!?!

I told myself that there should be no reason why I'd have to defend myself in another relationship. Neither would I be ignored. My parents are deceased and I had one child, on purpose. I had no intentions on raising another grown man. You wouldn't hear me out when I wanted to share my concerns. You would cut me off, disregard my feelings, and yet have the nerve to talk at me as if I was your child! Last I learned, you only have two, in which I wasn't any of them.

Things started to turn around for him and like any proud woman would be, I was supportive. He had a dilemma that would delay him returning back to work. You would never guess what it was… He was behind on making child support payments, and if he didn't get the matter resolved, his license would get suspended. You guessed it! But not entirely… I went to the county office and paid the bill myself. Got my receipt and waited to see how he would react.

He showed me how ungrateful he was. His foul mouth was fixed to cuss me for talking on the phone for more time than he cared for. I was too through! I knew I had to end this parasitic relationship. Counted my loss and told him that he didn't have to worry about paying me back. A peace of mind was much more important to me!

I see him from time to time and I'm glad to report that the two years since we've dated, he's a much more responsible man. While I still think about asking for my money back, its glad knowing that he's growing in the areas where he once lacked.

Please keep in mind that these are my encounters with men who I believe weren't quite ready for what they were asking for. I've been there too and will share that with you next. We all go through seasons of change. It's the cycle of life. There are good days, just as there are bad days. We change where and when we want to. Accepting people for who they are is a choice.

When a relationship didn't work out, I'd take as much time as I needed to reflect on self. Think about what I did to contribute to the outcome. I didn't beg a man to stay who wanted to leave. Nor did I keep one for the sake of having one. I date myself and enjoy my own company. That's actually a very healthy habit. There are moments I get concerned about how much I like me space and consider is it really necessary to have someone else share it.

Expressions of a Single Woman

You took my kindness for weakness.

Correction.

It was because of my kindness that I gave

unselfishly to you.

You cannot repay me by your words.

For your actions revealed was really in your

heart.

No more bitterness when I recall what's all been

lost.

I've gained wisdom to be more discerning when

anyone comes to me attempting to deceive by another

sad story...

Keeping Up Appearances

He noticed me during VBS. I was in my work clothes, wear a grey skirt, printed top, and peep toe pumps. My hair was curled and I was up front interacting with people from different groups. At this time, he was a leader in ministry, a divorced, militant man, who was also a public figure. I had no idea who he was, nor was I interested in getting his attention. The priority was to grow in faith and stay on the straight and narrow.

It gets lonely on that road after a while. I know my spirit was willing, but my flesh was getting weak. It's been nearly two years since I went on a date.

On the phone before getting out of my car to get some gas, I shared with one of my big sister's that I was ready to try it again. No sooner than the words left my mouth, someone shouts out to me from another pump, trying to get my attention. He says that he has a message for me. His face looked familiar, so I spent a brief moment hearing him out. He told me that I had a secret admire.

I didn't believe it for a second and let him know it too. He told me who the admirer was and my attitude instantly changed. I knew exactly who he was referring to then. Yet, if that man wanted to get to know who I was, he'd have to be the one to let me know himself. I didn't think that grown males still passed word through one another.

Right before he left for a mission's trip, my admirer let me know that he'd noticed me and wanted to learn more about me once he returned. I heard his request, but would occupy myself with school while he was away. As soon as he returned, the mating call was loud and clear.

Hear me well, men and women were created after the image of God. Every emotion that one feels is natural. However, those emotions are to stay within certain boundaries in order not to cause any drama. Men are indeed visual. If they're attracted to you, it's like the scent of their favorite meal. Most women like to hear a man who desires her. Very few guard their heart. It's lack of discipline that leaves them periodically in brokenness.

During the early courting stages of this relationship, I made it clear what the boundary lines were. He respected them. However, the more time we spent together, it was difficult keeping our flesh under subjection. Our carnal selves finally gave in. The flames that grew dim had were now full blaze.

I lived in two places and was most happy when I was away from home. I'd make sure that my home was kept and my son was fed, but I didn't want anyone to interrupt this season of passion. He was thoughtful and considerate. Candle lit bubble baths. Wine. Music. Clothes. Jewelry. Flowers. Home cooked meals where I didn't have to light the stove. I was treated as a woman who need not be in any other role than that when I was with him. If this was how he treated his lady, I wanted to be that for as long as I could.

Well, while I was splitting my time between homes, I had no idea that a storm was brewing. I was caught up in a whirlwind and there would be no shelter to cover me. I was happy, but blind to the fact that I was conforming once again to a man's need. I need you to wear this – so he bought it. You going to get your hair done – I hate weaves, but a cute little pixie cut like Halle Berry – ooh that's so much better! Why you trying to lose weight – I love your thickness. Never mind that I gained at least 3 dress sizes. Who was I? Hell if I knew!

I had the security code to the alarm system, plenty of space to keep my things, so I didn't have bring any clothes most time I stayed over. His initial behavior toward me made me feel like I was the best thing since slice bread… Yet, when it came time to worship together, I wasn't allowed in that space.

Well, I knew I was wrong for carrying one like a married woman who was very much single. I had forsaken my first love and there would be grave consequences to pay.

Redemption time would soon come, leaving me devastated. He had a guest in town, but still wanted me to visit. Bought a pizza and convinced me to come by. I drove all the way listening to music on the radio trying to drown out the sound of the Holy Spirit telling me to turn around and go home. I was convicted severely about the relationship. Yet it was my man that I wanted to please. My actions weren't pleasing to God.

Don't you know that when you put anything or anyone before God you could lose it all!?!

We ate, laughed, and made our way upstairs. I knew I should've left after I dinner, but I stayed. I took a shower and was planning on going right to bed. I gave the excuse that I was tired, but he wanted me. I laid next to me, but couldn't go through with it. Before anything else could happen, I got up out the bed, put my clothes on and left. No words were exchanged. We both knew we were wrong. Our sin had become habitual. The weight of it was too much for me. My soul ached! I had to get as far away as I could.

I cried for days, knowing I couldn't stay in a relationship that separated me further from God. I refused to continue to love a man who provoked me to sin. You said you loved me. I didn't doubt it. I just couldn't see it anymore. Lust is what moved you. I could see it in your eyes.

I was very much at fault! I knew what you liked and I hardly refused. I aimed to please, but the price was more than I could pay. You really didn't want me, at least not all of me.

His ego was bruised. He resented me. I abandoned him, but he quickly moved on. A week passes by and no words were exchanged. My girls knew the pain, but they couldn't offer any relief. They knew that I had to endure the discipline alone. My emotions were all over the place.

Out of anger, I grabbed everything he bought me, placed them in the trunk of my car, and drove to his house. He had already had company to help heal his hurt. I was disgusted, but I was no longer in denial about the truth.

I had to find me again! I didn't recognize who I had become. I lost myself along the way. No matter how long it would take, I had to get back to me.

After spending a year in counseling, I would emerge a new me. The reason for getting help was because I had to find out why I reacted the way that I did, why would I hold onto things, then explode... The life issues that I shared was that of toxic relationships and people pleasing. I would hardly say no. I was afraid of rejection and disturbing the peace.

Thank God, I was an active participant in this delivery mission! It took time to heal, but I knew not to rush the process. I had to drop off the weighty baggage that I picked up along the way. I didn't want to chance missing out on a new opportunity by bringing the old into a new relationship. It's so unfair to try and make other pay for the faults of others.

Letting go isn't easy, but holding onto to negative behavior and unhealthy relationships, contribute to the deterioration of your soul. New seasons require purging, and getting rid of things that aren't needed, in preparation for what you've been waiting for or desire most. It's worth it to yourself to start from scratch.

Expressions of a Single Woman

I tried to become who you wanted me to be.

Yet still, that was never enough.

When I looked in the mirror, my own reflection I could not see.

My flesh was marred, once smooth, and now rough.

You cared more about what others would say if they'd seen us together,

Instead of boldly professing that we were indeed lovers.

Through the tears and the pain, I learned to set boundaries,

Let my voice be heard,

And to respect my needs carefully above others.

My Homey, Brother, Friend

We met almost twenty years ago from mutual friends. We were about that life! Both had personal struggles, but we were friends who looked out for one another. At a critical time, you were hidden from me. But when God saw fit, He'd bring us back together again. It seemed to be that way for us for years.

When I moved back to Georgia thirteen years ago, I was out on a date at a movie theater. We noticed each other from opposite sides of the room. Like a scene from a movie, we ran toward each other, embracing and laughing. We exchanged contact information, promising to catch up another time. My poor date was confused. He was sure I had got him caught up in some mess. I let him know that it was just an old friend.

When we did see each other again, he said he had some news to share. I was certain that he married his girlfriend from our old church.

Well, he stops by my place and pulls a chair away from the table, asking me to sit down and be quiet. He then proceeds to bend down on one knee to propose. I sat in the chair stunned!

Then my blood boiled. I jumped out the chair and told him how insulted I was. Mind you, he was still with ole girl, just like I thought. I was angry at him for her. I let him know I wasn't interested, and I and my son deserved better. I also told him that he had to leave.

Once he left, I laughed... That is not how I envisioned a marriage proposal. The nerve of him to think that he could just show up, empty handed at that, and act like those words, that many women want to hear - would woo me!?! Absolutely not!

He eventually decided to marry his long-time girlfriend. I sincerely wished them well.

We remain close friends to this day. He is like a big brother who has been supportive of me and my family over the years. He is still very vocal when it comes to expressing his feelings. I remind him sometimes that his words are useless if he doesn't act on them. A single mother doesn't want a grown man to show up empty handed with a mouth full of empty promises! Show me what you're talking about!

I'm not saying that you shouldn't date a friend. There are couples out there that have successful relationships. Being friends was a vital part of their foundation. I caution you. For the friend you think you know can be completely different when that boundary line has been crossed.

I Really Love This Man

Case in point...

Working in an office with ninety percent woman can be a bit much. When the voice or scent of a man is near, we all take notice.

About twelve years ago, I heard an unfamiliar voice coming from the front office. I just had to see who it belonged to. Before I made it out front, I took a minute to straighten my hair and clothes. I was wearing a fuchsia pink blended top, black slim fit pants, and pink stilettos. When this handsome man saw me, his response about my appearance made me blush. I opened the front door and went to the ladies room, glad about the reaction I had just received.

Several days had passed and my coworker let me know that it was her brother who stopped by. She apologized for his blunt behavior. Then let me know that he said it was okay to give me his number. I waited another day before I called him. I didn't want to seem too anxious, but I was elated! We spoke for a brief moment and made plans to go to out over the weekend.

For our first date, I wore a cream colored halter jumpsuit and sandals. My hair was curled, and I wore simple jewelry and light perfume. I wanted to make another good impression. He was the perfect gentleman. Having dinner and a movie turned out to be a good night. Before parting ways, we agreed that we'd like to see each other again...

Although our relationship seemed to change like the seasons over the years, he has watched me grow tremendously. He was there through times of celebration - when I purchased my first home. Also through times of sorrow - losing my mother. He has been a good example to my son as well.

He is a hardworking, giving, and caring man. He is bold and brave. He loves his family and is a loyal friend. How could a woman not fall in love with a man like this?

This one particular season brought us back together. Neither of us were in a relationship with anyone else. He called to ask for some help with starting a new business venture. I agreed without hesitation. It's always great to see your friends succeed! After taking care of a few administrative tasks for him, he invited me to breakfast to say thank you. We used that time to catch up with one another. With our stomachs full and laughter on our lips, we made it to our cars to go our separate ways. I purposed that day, I'd be sure to not let so much time pass by before seeing him again.

True to the promise I made, I started to check in with him frequently. We would spend more time together. Being mature and knowing what I wanted at this stage of my life, I shared with him how I felt, and what were my intentions, and expectations. He didn't disagree with me, but he didn't agree to what I said either. We sort of fell back into a pattern of convenience. I didn't want to take the time to meet and learn someone new, so I stayed and dealt with what was familiar.

One night when we were together, I poured my heart out to him, letting him know that I wanted to be married, and to him. He listened, then responded loudly in silence. I knew then it was time to let go. Only thing, our souls were tied together in knots.

I knew what he didn't say that night, so I started to distance myself in order to heal. I had to prepare myself for what I really wanted.

Instead of focusing on who didn't want me and any other negative thing, I put energy into being better for me. I didn't want to meet someone else that had potential and not be ready. I purposed getting rid of the excess baggage of past hurts and failures. I became more active in self-care. I'd date me again and be happy in the process. I'd treat myself to dinner, see a movie, shop, and even go to a concert to listen to some live jazz.

It was fun falling in love with myself again! Enjoying my own company for hours. Being content with not having to compromise in order to have companionship. My self-confidence was restored. My faith also grew stronger. I took a long look in the mirror and told myself that I am beautiful, intelligent, and a blessing to the lives of many. So, instead of fretting about what couldn't be, I accepted what was, and make the most of what is.

I'd rather not stay where I'm not wanted. Not being chosen by the one who I thought would choose me doesn't mean that I'm undesirable, it means that we both have a choice to exercise our own free wills. I've come to realize now, that I have to be a priority. Being convenient no longer works for me. It's all or nothing! It's all day, every day, including weekends, holidays, and all special occasions, with family and friends, through the good, bad, and indifferent days - for the rest of our lives...

Ladies, our intentions and expectations have to be clear up front. State your wants and needs. Don't be afraid to communicate! Set standards and impose consequences. Feelings may get hurts and egos may get bruised. Let those moments be opportunities to grow in grace and humility. If we keep moving the boundary lines, they'll continue to be crossed, and no one will take you seriously.

If you're not in a committed relationship, use this time to become a better version of yourself. Take the time to be, do, create, and live your sweet, best, and redefined life. So when the next opportunity comes your way, you'll be ready for it. If you don't like what you're attracting, look within, and be honest about what's there and change it. You shouldn't expect from others what you won't even give yourself. Like you! Love you! Flaws and all!

Short. Tall. Dark. Light. Black. White. American. Christian. Muslim. Catholic. American. Caribbean. English. Spanish. Wealthy. Affluent. Broke. Hood. Educated. Frugal. Needy. Young. Old. Exceptional credit. No credit. Missing teeth. Dentures. AAA. AARP. Yessss, all the above and in between.

You have laughed until you cried. Made promises that you broke repeatedly. You let him go, and let him come back in. You are what you accept! Take ownership of your life, make some adjustments, and live out life satisfied without further regret. Be okay starting over, and enjoy the journey.

Everyone who comes into your life will either have something to give you or take something away from you. If you're willing to exercise patience and self-control, the exchange can actually turn out to be a valuable one. Your presence will leave a lasting impression.

Dating Without Discrimination

As Believers, we're told to be specific with our prayers. That I am! Yet, once I've poured my heart out to God, I submit all my desires to Him, asking and trusting that His will be done. My loving Father knows me very well. He hand crafted me to be a unique individual, an express image of Himself.

I have loved easy and hard. My heart, even though I know it should be guarded - like Fort Knox - loves to love. Out of that love, I've given to all who crossed my path without expecting much in return. That character flaw has been a source of pain. Pain felt to my soul, by the rejection, abandonment, and abuse.

In all honesty and transparency, I still believe in love. I was created from it. It's knit into my entire being. Now, I exercise wisdom, discernment, and caution. When I meet someone, I am open about my interests and expectations. Does that leave room for disappointment? Certainly! But, I can't begin anything, even a new relationship with a negative mindset.

Life has taught me many things. By the grace of God, I'll continue being a lifelong learner. Not only that, but I'll also keep working at it until it works out for me. I admit that I wanted to give up on love countless times. I've said that it was too hard, it shouldn't hurt, and wondered why it was taking so long!?!

Loving people is hard! We are fleshly beings who without the spirit of God and His constant influence, can display such wickedness that takes another life out of pride, envy, and hatred. So instead of giving into that nature, I'm committed to loving, even those who appear to be unlovable.

Love hurts worse than a toothache and labor pains combined to the tenth degree. Yet, there is joy in and after the pain. God loved us so much that he sacrificed His only Son, Jesus. There's no doubt that it hurt beyond words could explain. Sometimes you can't explain love - the how or whys. Love is not so much what you say, but what you do. Just as faith without works is dead. Love that does not act or do, is hard to believe.

Finally, it takes a lifetime to love. I am forty-one years young and grateful to have made it thus far! I've experienced the love as a daughter, sister, mother, and friend. Each relationship brought something different.

I believe that I too have rejected others and made myself at times to be unlovable... by having, displaying negative and destructive attitude and behaviors. I've also conformed myself into what others wanted me to be in fear of my love not being reciprocated.

Withholding love isn't right! It's something so precious that we received and not deserved. Knowing that deep in my soul helps me to continue to love. No longer do I have to take offense when others don't choose me. Their decision doesn't mean I should take it personal. One of the most beautiful things that I've learned was to accept and love myself. For all that I am, have been, and will ever be...

I LOVE ME SOME ME!!!

Expressions of a Single Woman

Be not afraid to love again, nor let them love you.

The words in your heart come directly out of your mouth, and so often do you call their name.

How I desire to be thought of in that way and loved sincerely too...

No Longer Afraid

(Hodge, N. 2018, December 12)

For some time all I knew was loss

Until I came to realize that all of life costs

Food, clothing, and shelter are basic necessities

But when you're without, the lack brings you to your knees

So out of fear I became aggressive with my search

From career, economic status, love interests, and the

church

It wasn't until I obtained and achieved many hearts desires

That part of me knew there was no more need to acquire

Oh how foolish I felt once I poured out my heart

When all I wanted was genuine love from the very start

I have no regrets of giving myself for real this time around

Neglect and rejection proved painful, but through it more
of me I have I found
Even if you choose to ignore the words that have been said
Do remember this one thing,

I am **NO LONGER AFRAID!**

To love. To lose. Remain open to finding the truth...
Knowing that I am worth it is enough proof
So no more holding on to someone who doesn't want to be
kept
Now I make myself available to the one who has depth
Of wisdom, knowledge, heart and soul
Agreeing to walk together as the ultimate goal

The End of a New Beginning

I have a better understanding of relationships and what my role is in each of them. Not everyone wants or needs something from me. Some are allowed to give into my life. It does help to pray for discernment, to clearly know that I don't have to receive what is being brought to me.

While I've been rejected, abandoned, neglected, appeared to some as not quite enough, said to be the best thing, but only to be kept a secret, or forgotten of, even ignored and considered a shame in public, loved and hated all in the same day... I do not fault them. Nor do I have any ill will against them.

As a young adult, I had a brief encounter with the man who raped me as a teenager. He apologized to me for what he did, and I've forgiven him.

Through the process of dating, I've met some pretty outstanding people. Collected much data that I can use in the future or pass it on to someone else who may encounter a character trait of whom I already met.

Our encounters were for a season. Some shorter than others. None that I've met thus far was intended to be my life mate. I've learned to have better standards, clearly communicate my desires and wants, as well as omitting somethings that weren't as important that I initially thought.

Some have gone on to marry… Congratulations! Some are still out there playing the field. I pray that they are well and that they will indeed find what they are looking for. No love lost...

The time that I've spent unmarried, has given me the opportunity to do all that I desire to do, and without much interruption. I can give my undivided attention to what's at hand. I have resolved that if I don't marry, it's absolutely okay. I can continue to be successful, and master my God-given gifts. It is with those gifts that I can add and multiply.

COMING TO THE CROSS©

A Personal Journey of Salvation

Table of Contents

1. Where it all began

I remember getting on a bus that came through our neighborhood on Sundays to take us to church. As time passed we no longer went by bus. My mom would walk with us. It was far, but we were accustomed to walking. We attended Sunday school where we learned about the bible from a child's perspective.

There would be a break in between services. Sometimes we'd walk to the store to get candy before heading back for worship service. We tried to sit still and listen to what was being shared, but it didn't always work that way.

I enjoyed going to church! We spent a lot of time there, so we made the most of it. From bible study on Wednesdays to serving food to those in need on Saturdays, this became a regular part of my life. This is what we did!

One Sunday, when I was around seven years old, I made a decision about my salvation. Learning about Jesus was exciting and I was certain I wanted Him to be a part of my life. My mom made sure that I understood what I was doing. I did! Not to say that

I felt different, but I knew something in me had changed. My mom also shared with me that because of my decision to accept Christ, I was different. I changed and wouldn't be like everyone else. Now that part I wouldn't understand for quite some time.

Not long after answering the call to salvation, I got baptized. Again, I was asked if I understood my decision. I did!

I liked to kneel at the altar, to pray. Praying for my family or whatever was on my heart. I believed that God listened to me.

I asked permission to join the children's choir. It was fun to see them wear their robes and march down the aisle. My mom let me sing in the choir, but not before sharing that by doing so would be a sacrifice. I'd learn about what that really meant soon enough.

Since we spent a lot of time there, I wanted to be involved. I also thought it was kind to help others in need. God took care of us, so we should want to treat people how He treats us.

After a while, time with friends grew scarce. It seemed like there was a lot of responsibility, and there was... but I wanted to return to not being so busy and just be a kid. I didn't want to be at church all the time… Yet, my mom taught me at young age to honor your commitments, or to not make them at all.

There were also times we would visit with other women from the church. At their homes, we'd sing, pray, and read the bible there too. It was during a home visit that I received my first bible. If other kids were there on the nights we came, we could have a little fun. Maybe color, or if it wasn't too dark, we could go outside to play.

In the summers, there was vacation bible school or VBS. That was a fun time for all the kids. The adults made sure we learned about biblical principles, but enjoyed the process too. Outside of occasionally having bible study at different homes, we rarely visited other churches. We became like a blended family. I sang in the children's choir for a few years and stayed at the church until I moved away after graduating from high school.

11. Prodigal Child

From the time of my acceptance of Jesus as my personal Savior and moving to another country and state, I had many life challenges.

I ran away from home and got into lots of trouble. I was saved, but lived a carnal, and careless life. There were times of discipline that would cause me walk on the straight and narrow, but there were a lot of inconsistencies. I wasn't feeding my spirit in order to grow stronger with my faith.

Curiosity about many things caused me to be easily influenced. I didn't go to church as often as I did as a young child. I now had a choice, and I'd exercise my free will as much as I'd like.

I was a long distance runner for a semester in high school and my life was turning out to be that way too. I had a child out of wedlock. Guilt set it. Yet, I thought I was grown for having a child. Then realizing, I wasn't ready to parent because I too was still a child.

I've since made peace with my mom from being a rebellious child, causing her much pain. I needed her help! I thought I failed her and God! She encouraged me by letting me know that she wasn't ashamed of me. She also let me know that it was okay to simply talk to God. There would be nothing that I could do that would take Him by surprise.

My mother was there for me greatly in the area of my spiritual growth. She was my mom, but also a spiritual mother and mentor in Christ. She disciplined me much as a child, but when she would disciple me out of love, my heart was ready to receive it.

I had a difficult time understanding how to guard my heart, and that made me become prey for the attacks of enemy.

III. The Reality of Spiritual Warfare

Just like Jesus was tempted, so will we be. There have been times when I could see the attack coming. I'd consecrate myself and be ready to battle. Then there would be moments when I'd be so unaware. Blindsided by a sucker punch. It didn't have to evaluate the damage. Any blow the enemy could throw, it would be enough to shift my stance.

I admit to leaving doors open because of my lack of self-control and wanting to please my flesh. The enemy would pounce on my, trying best to steal my last breath.

God is strategic in the way He moves. Just study the account of Creation. The enemy isn't as foolish as some may think. He studies us. Watches our every move. So he can run back to God to accuse us. He sets traps. Using anger and unforgiveness as bait. I was angry for a very long time. At life, people, and circumstances... Holding onto anger for so long, I was a fool. I was defensive. Took things way too personal. If others didn't react for being slighted, I'd appoint myself to be offended for them. This gave the enemy plenty of ammunition to destroy me. He'd throw lies at me, which I'd start to believe. I'd doubt what I knew to be true. I'd get confused over elementary things.

The greatest attack was on my mind. I was saved, but mentally sick. My relationship with my Savior was strained, but not severed. I believe like how Saul had a distressing spirit from God on him, it was allowed to be upon me too. Not to destroy me, but to bring me to a place where God could redeem me.

I was a prodigal child, far away from the protective covering of a church home. Out living a not so holy life, and my heart was hard and turning ice cold. That is not what God had planned for me! However, He let me fall flat on my face, to humble me. I took life for granted, as if I deserved it. While I was in the hospital, my eyes and ears were opened. Deliverance was available to me, but did I want it!?! Absolutely!

I wanted to live! I wanted my mind restored! I didn't want to learn elementary things all over again! The Lord released me, redeemed me from the hands of the enemy. He brought me safely home to recover. He assured me that - it indeed is well with my soul!

However, I had to do my part. I had to fight for my life! Crucifying my flesh, multiple times each day. Spend unlimited in the Word, feeding my spirit so it can be healthy and strong. It wasn't enough to just study the Word, but I had to put it into action. It was a rough process, but God's strength was certainly made perfect in all of my weaknesses. The attacks of the enemy on my life are frequent, but not be as severe as that day. I am on a hit list. The assigns whomever he can to catch me off guard, so he can cut me move in again for the kill.

A time of vulnerability would come again when my mother passed. I lost a mother, mentor, and friend. I was devastated! I literally told God, "I'll be back!" I didn't know where I was going, but I knew I needed time to cool off. He wanted to comfort me, and I let Him, just not for too long. I'd enjoy peace, but then forfeit it because I was hurting. I knew my mom was resting, in peace, without pain, or suffering. Who was going to pray for me!?! Who was going to advise me on parenting my son!?! She's not going to see me marry!?!

I wept many times from the depths of my soul! The Lord allowed me to weep and walk by the not so still waters. When He seen that I was straying too far away, He draw me back to Him. He listened to my fears, my cries, my dreams... I searched His Word for at least one promise that would sustain me. He gave me plenty! He kept His Words and recaptured my heart - just as He did when I was seven years old.

IV. Religion and Relationship

Religion taught me about rules that kept me constantly in a state of guilt. That if I didn't follow them, or get something all the way right, I was a failure. "You didn't go to church, prayer meeting, and attend bible study this week. Are you sure you saved?" "You're not serving in at least three ministries, pulling your weight at home, and you were late again to work! And you call yourself a Christian!?!"

Religion creates restrictions. Makes you busy with so many activities - where you don't even have enough time to pray or read your own bible, and then makes you feel guilty about it all.

Relationship is where you can connect and create a bond. You can be yourself and not fear rejection. You can admit your faults and still be accepted. You can exchange your burdens and weaknesses. You can accept discipline out of love. You can be liberated while you aren't yet free. You can know that Jesus sacrificed His life in your place, and caused you to be an heir that reaps all the benefits and inheritance that you never deserved. He can also relate to everything you will ever go through, and love you still.

Truth: I attend corporate worship services weekly to collectively fellowship with a body of believers, be encouraged, and refuel to continue a daily life of service, out on the battlefield... I don't go to church. I am the church!

Lord,

I thank You for deliverance from religion. For reminding me that the relationship I have with You is more valuable than attending every meeting in a building with a cross on the roof. Thank You for teaching me about Kingdom business, which is humbly serving the people You created. Thank You for the freedom to worship in spirit and in truth, even in the comforts of home, at work, or wherever You are. Thank You for an opportunity to hear Your voice, through Your Spirit, guiding me every step of each day... I Love You! In the Name of Jesus! Amen

V. I'm saved and I know I'm saved!

Long ago, my steps were ordered by the Lord. I am a sinner, saved by grace. I shouldn't habitually sin, but sin less because of my relationship with Jesus Christ. I should live to please Him - not others or even myself.

Each day, I purpose to monitor the condition of my heart. If what is coming from my mouth is foul, then I know I need to hide away in the presence of God, and get a good soul washing.

As a disciple, I want to represent my savior, Jesus, well. I don't want the personal issues that I haven't dealt with be the cause of someone faltering or going astray. It's a beauty that I have healthy relationship with people to hold me accountable, even with my spiritual life.

In all honesty, being a Christian isn't easy! It takes much effort on your part. When you fall, get back up. You will have to suffer. Be it loss in a relationship or of material positions. Your faith will be tested. But, YOU WILL MAKE IT!

I am committed to serve! Not by eloquent words that some won't understand, but daily, in practical ways. Remembering how I've been blessed, and try best to be that – do that for someone else. Bearing good fruit that will remain. Praying not by pressure, but out of sincere passion. Serving everywhere. Even when no one is looking or there is no gratitude given. It is a lifestyle, and one that I'm most proud to live!

AMEN

About the Author

Nichelle A. Hodge, although having suffered through much abuse has remained committed to her faith, supportive of those who cross her path, and strives every day to live her life in excellence and victory. Nichelle is a daughter, mother, sister, and friend. Also an author, artist, educator, and consultant. She is committed to a life of service. She enjoys cooking, reading, writing, and traveling. These days, she also enjoys $5 Movie Tuesdays, and designing comforting creations through her business Fruit Blankets. She is available for speaking engagements and to facilitate small group classes that encourage the growth of women in the Kingdom, body of Christ.

www.ingramcontent.com/pod-product-compliance
Lightning Source LLC
Chambersburg PA
CBHW071940190726
48293CB00004B/1291

* 9 7 8 1 9 7 0 0 7 9 5 1 7 *